HΔIKU
HIGH COOL
HI KOOL

written by Derrick Standifer
Illustrated by Jasmine Standifer
Cover art by Tellis Rodgers

What Is a Haiku?

Haikus are of Japanese origin and are composed of seventeen syllables in three lines. The first line is five syllables, the second line is seven syllables, and the third line is five syllables. Usually Haikus juxtapose two images or ideas using wit, pun, and other poetry elements. The haikus in this book covers a range of topics from social injustices to religion. Some of these Haikus are my attempt at play on words, some are short stories, and others are words of encouragement. Many are comical. I am optimistic that these Haikus bring you as much joy as I have had writing them. Enjoy, and hopefully they inspire you to compose haikus of your own.

White men can't **jump** is

a lie. If you don't believe

me ask Rodney King.

SEGREGATION should

only be allowed when there's

ALCOHOL involved.

There is a direct

correlation with **sagging**

pants and **sagging** dreams.

Cigarettes are the

leading cause of **DEATH**, yet **WEED**

is what's illegal.

■ ■

You expect me to

worship when *preachers* do stuff

I'd go to *hell* for .

You expect me to

obey when *police* do stuff

I'd go to *jail* for.

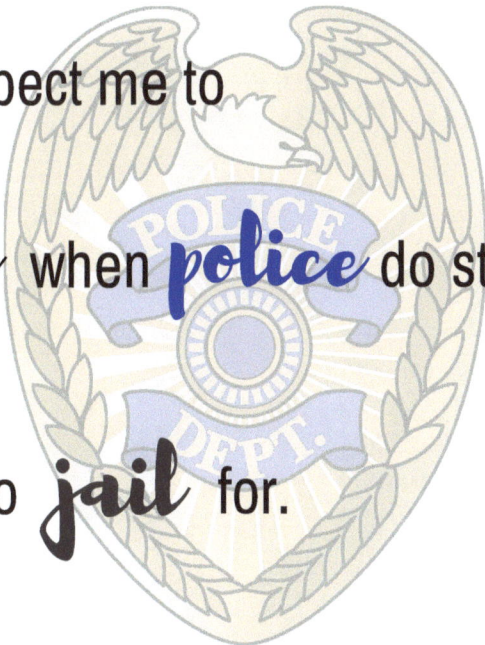

3

Being *touched* by a *preacher* used to be a good thing till *Eddie Long*.

What would you do if your *virgin wife* came in and said she was *pregnant?*

BRAINWASH our people

through the use of RELIGION:

CHRISTIANITY.

If a **DOG** was to

look in a mirror they would

most likely see **GOD**

One day you're going

to **wake up** old then one day

you just won't **wake up.**

World *religions* are

fighting a *battle* over

who is more *peaceful.*

Don't *lie* to yourself

if you *lie* to yourself then

you will *lie* to God.

The #1 key

to gaining SUCCESS is to

mind your own business

Do not lose a friend over money. Lose a friend over a compass.

Nature provides the talent, but *hard work* is what provides the *success*.

I never did think
that being **negative** could
be so **positive**.

April showers ain't
got nothing on a poet's
brainstorming power.

GOOD THINGS HAVE NEVER GONE TO THOSE WHO WAIT. GOOD THINGS GO TO THOSE WHO WORK .

If you *dream* just a

little bit then you will get

to *live* life a lot.

◆◆◆◆◆◆◆◆◆◆◆◆◆

The *key* to getting *rich* is not cutting back. It's making more *money* .

Good friends got your BACK.

Great FRIENDS will take what's on their back and GIVE to you.

When **lost** in a crowd you'll see **everyone** except who you're **looking** for.

AS SOON AS I **walked**

ACROSS THE **stage** THERE WERE **loan**

collectors WAITING.

Pens and **pencils** in

palms possessing people to

become some **poets.**

We SPEND too much on

Being FRESH and not enough

on not SPOILING .

13

Half the people **die**

from **starvation** the other

half **obesity** .

More **money** being

spent on the **outside** of the

body than the **in** .

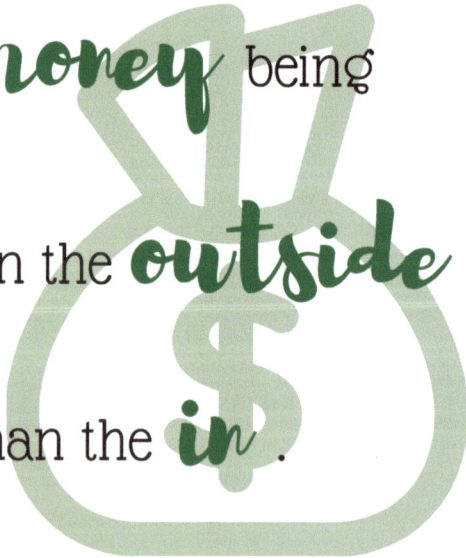

To the *mother* on the Marta bus: a *diaper* is not an *outfit*.

If you want to be **charged** to have your life **saved** then go to a **doctor**.

Facebook will allow me to know your life story before I know you.

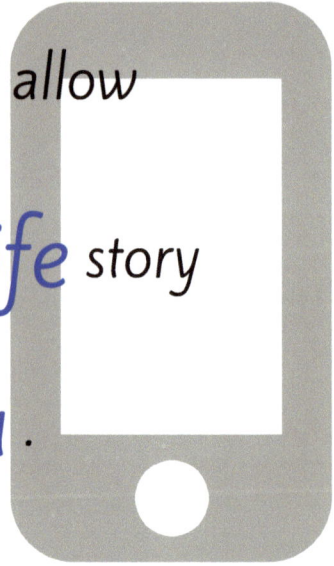

Republicans and Democrats are foes until the world's not watching.

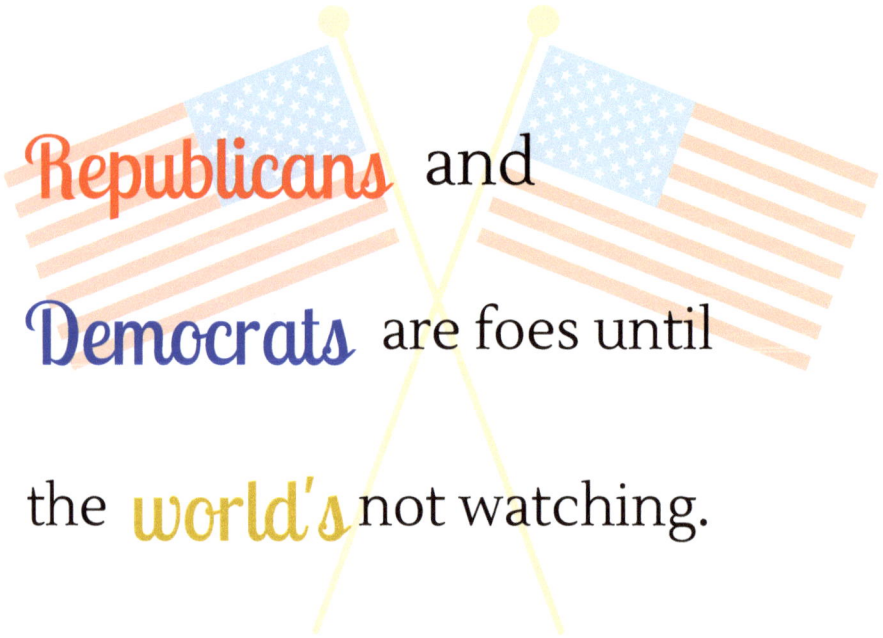

A red and white cane.

a real fly ride with 3 hoes.

Santa is a pimp.

~~~~~~~~~~~~~~~~~~~~~~~

Social Media

got some thinking that they are

social activists.

~~~~~~~~~~~~~~~~~~~~~~~

I have a **SIX PACK**

just lacking the **PLASTIC** things

that **HOLDS** them in place.

Go **HAM** does not mean

hard as a **motherfucker**.

It means **cheer** for **babe**.

I told my foreign

exchange student to hit the

lights; she punched the wall.

· ·

My nurse has more swag

than anyone that I know.

I call her kool-aid.

· ·

Happy *Father's Day*

I got my *mother* a card.

she taught me to *pee* .

If you just got to

include your 2 cents then why

don't you pay it all.

Marta gained one more customer when gas hit $4 dollars a gallon.

I do not mind if

I lose a foot race. A dog

will never catch me.

||||||||||||||||||||||||||||||||||||

If you are going

to **sag** at least wear some **draws**

with no **doo doo** stains.

||||||||||||||||||||||||||||||||||||

The ONLY thing that

makes us DOMINANT is the

OPPOSABLE thumb.

Proof that **roaches** are

nocturnal : when I turn on

the lights they **scatter** .

My *mama* said I

brought you in. I'll take you out.

Casey Anthony

Man he really knows

his style of *hare*. He must have

owned a *rabbit* farm.

The early *bird* is

who catches the *worm*, but what

if the *worm* was late?

I like **converses**

because they are **16 bars**

behind **16 bars** .

Is it possible

for a midget to get high

on marijuana?

I *hate* it when I

flush the toilet and *doo doo*

comes back afterward.

Ninety nine bottles

of beer on the wall. Damn they

must have been some drunks .

If your *head* hurts then

you should stop using your *teeth*

during *oral sex*.

Having got the **draws**

don't mean we had **sex**. It means

I can't **win** or **lose**.

I only have *safe*

sex. Do you have protection?

I brought my *helmet*.

Firefighters and

pimps have the same job. Both are

known for pulling **hoes**.

I don't go to **strip**

clubs because **pornos** are free,

and they can **rewind** .

If my mom liked blow

pop instead of peanuts, then

I wouldn't be here.

29

It is make believe

you need *Maybelline* to look

like a *beauty queen* .

Chess is just like life.

queens do all the work, yet the

kings get the credit.

She has to be a

student at FAMU the way

she rocking those heels.

Women will never

be free till the downfall of

man ain't blamed on Eve .

31

If I was **Jack** in

the Titanic **Rose** would have

had to **move** over.

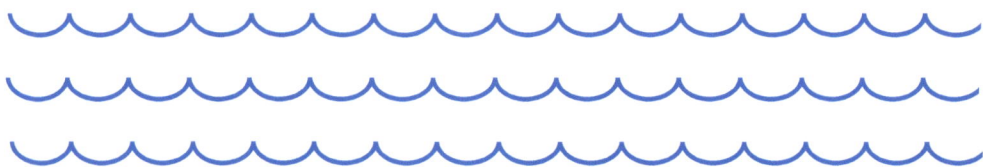

My *wife* always wants

me to be *romantic* but

I am not *Roman*.

If I *love* you and

only you, then what about

the *other letters*?

Many are *born* in

November, *9 months* before

is *Valentine's Day.*

A guy with *no ears,* and a girl with a *big mouth* are a *perfect match.*

www.ingramcontent.com/pod-product-compliance
Lightning Source LLC
Chambersburg PA
CBHW041759040426
42447CB00001B/25